About the author

Vernon Tungsten Sullivan was born in Ireland. He grew up in Dublin, and worked in numerous menial jobs before he left Ireland to travel extensively.

He spent twenty years teaching English and writing for magazines in South East Asia and then South America.

His first novel, *Hexpectations* was published in 2002 and a collection of short stories entitled *Right You Be* followed in 2006. He has recently published two collections of novellas, *Besides* and *Harry Keighery*. (Both 2014)

He is married with two children, and divides his time between Ireland and south America.

This is his first poetry collection.

By the same author:

HEXPECTATIONS

RIGHT YOU BE

BESIDES

HARRY KEIGHERY

The Age of Aquarius:
Teenage Poems

by Vernon T. Sullivan

First published 2014.

ISBN 978-1-291-73444-7

For Mam

Author's Note

I wrote these poems between the ages of twelve and about fifteen. The only exceptions to this are the poems 'Poem written on the street' and 'Flashback' which were written when I was eighteen or nineteen, but the poetry mania had already passed.

The poems are printed chronologically, so the reader might see the development---if any---that occurs from start to finish. Many poems have been lost, or not included because I couldn't find the finished version, only the earlier drafts, and I know how meticulous the fourteen year old me would've been in insisting that unfinished poems didn't go in.

That age when the mind is opening up, and ravenous for information and curiosity of every kind. The love of sound and rhyme and melody. Of Hopkins and Blake in particular. Writing poems was a secret pleasure, and I told almost no-one about it, except the occasional like-minded or sympathetic soul who didn't mock my youthful endeavours. Those early teenage years in my upstairs bedroom in Kilgarve. The endless concentration I put into changing a word here, or adding a word there. The spiral-rimmed notebooks & the bewildering crossing-out and scribbling over.

I remember a woman called Winnie McKenna giving me a vinyl record. I think it was called *Dylan Thomas: Reading in New York* or something like that. The cut-glass accent, the impassioned delivery, the sound and lilt of his beautiful booming voice. I listened to it over and over again. Thanks, Winnie.

Perhaps the poems seem naive, or overly idealistic, but it's nice nonetheless to be able to give them a home somewhere. I can only laugh at the deep seriousness with which some of them (particularly the early ones) are written. The almost puritanical seriousness. The high-dudgeoned earnestness.

Others are almost criminally derivative, and chock full of unselfconscious adolescent vim and vigour. The reader might notice that in some poems apostrophes are included, while in others, they are not. I didn't make any changes to the poems, they go in from the handwritten or typed pages of youth directly. Others have been omitted, or only partially included. One, a thirty page poem about an experience with magic mushrooms has been left out. Likewise, a very long poem about killing a rabbit with myxomatosis called *The Stoning of the Leper* has only a fragment of the poem included. Also, *The Workhouse* was written before the advent of PC.

You can see that I was playing around with form and style in many different ways. To finally see them in print would have pleased the young boy. Sitting in a cool, dark room while the summer sun shone outside, I'm sure he would have liked it.

VTS, Feb 2014

In the gulag Archipelago
or Fiery Montevideo
I coulda bin long time ago
but may never know

In Mandarin,
or any other twistered tongue
the he that is also I
Could be writing this very poem
& on this very line.

If you want something done
ask a busy management
Cos laziness loiters lonely
what should
Shouldn't stay & lie there
only
A stale plan.

After bathing
& in the snug glow
of fresh new vigour
looks through her mirror
feels the warmth
of passion's fire
& burns in the embers
of her own desire.

The elixir of life
it held me for an age
when I was lost and didn't care
life as utopia's page

When I was hidden as the leaves
splayed content in mire of mirth
I languished Eden's renegade
A secret spy of earth.

Wasting in my room
tapping to a tune
TV throws discarded soons
as tree-topped shadows
trace the moon

Downstairs once more
She sits forlorn
brandishing a cigarette
Then animated--

Sighs her lifetime took
An extra between work
an autobiography
Coffee-tabled book

Never written--
just talk.

Servers Party.

Like the scream of a butterfly,
children are abused by those who
Misuse the use the bible issues--
A sordid metamorphosis into adult life.

But are not the Divine Emissaries
Victimised culprits of cloistered lust
repressed in infallible thrall?

Anachronistic eunuchs
Human enough to fall.
Child, 'guilty' victim of a life well slain,
Was it a lesson in catechism or masochism
An earthly Calvary of misplaced blame.

The Workhouse

Lesley Cod-Fishbone, oh Lesley Cod-Fishbone
As his dear Mum would say
Had better go look for a job
So out he did go
Helped by plea, bribe & foe
& rosaries offered to god.

Chances were slim, fat as he was
with 'Sorry, unsuitable' and the dreary 'because'
still hope he possessed
To succeed, out of need
& give his lone suit a well-deserved rest

Sure he waddn't no fool
for he went not to school
but two at a time if you may
When school bells did din
This scholar'd grin
& bring in the dough in the time-honoured way

No house, bank or boat
Least the ones still afloat

Could lie safe in the hours of dark
for with inquisitive eyes
& tools locks to prise
“Why, it's (Cod) Fishbone the criminal shark!”

But rumours do sail on anonymous waters,
From wool-weavin' grannies,
to poor milkman's daughters,
Like an ill-smelling scent
His name went before him
Giving employers a chance top deplore him
and a means to express their resent

Now sick of the trying
& the clear blatant lying
He felt he should call it a day
But Mum would have none
from her dog-lazy son
In her house at least she held sway

Devised was a plan
from bedridden Nan
using the toilet unable to flush

racking her brain
Yes, the one deemed insane
whilst spilling the bedpan
& its foul-smelling mush!

An argument followed at the family table
a woodworm's idea of a feast
Mum acknowledging this
With a sigh & a hiss:
"Well, somebody's workin at least!"

Through shouting & roars
& reddening sores
came like a thunderous cry from a fable
"You're lazy & fat
You do-nothing brat
You'll try 'slong as yer bloody-well able!"

And then uncle Joe
less a friend than a foe
Would donate his valued advice
"Well y'can try, & try twice
But it ain't hard to figure

They ain't on their knees offering work
To a fat, lazy, nogoodnik nig***"

The plan had arrived
Cunningly contrived
That put his many earrings to use
after each failured try
One more he could hide
All gone?
He might as well take to the noose!

So across London city
He'd have to get gritty
Any opening he couldn't deny
Well they still wouldn't listen
more earrings gone missing
"God help me, I'm too young to die!!"

The last chance of all
in the corner of the mall
lay little O'Flaherty's pub
A barman pouring a Guinness
& gaping with menace

"Y'Oirish?"
"Yeah, I'm a Dub"

That night it was clear
to tumultuous cheer
that at last she was proud
even speaking aloud
of the only black barman
in an Irish pub
in England
with 26 holes & an ear!

Tasted in the bowels
of the earth,
on trampled soil
mixed with mirth of yore
on which we standstill
today's floor, yesterday's land

Night watchmen
in lighthouses
guard the shore
from ships & nothingness.
Sentinels of silence.

The stars, a merrigoround
of lover's dark filmy dreams
cat whiskers, bats
& night screams.

Legs & arms
heartbeats charmed
huddled in the sweet
squirms of slumber

swam in numbers
& faces, strange places

the stream flows

Wind & thieves, aware their own
breath, living through death
as whispers
under windows.

Hawk or dove?

Watching television w/ a nature lover,
I suddenly wonder,
Is he a well-meaning dove
or moral hawk a-plunder.

Member of greenpeace, the RSPCA
& other benevolent agents
of sweet F.A

doesn't wear leather—the hide
of dead animals
strict vegan---the flesh
of dead animals
No deodorant---animal tested
Nor circuses---they're abused & molested!

A teardrop gives his eye
a saddened gleam
as a harpooned whale floods the screen
"Those dirty fucken Japs!
If I had a gun,
I'd loveta shoot them all"

I'm on excellent terms with the Universe
Walking wild
Through a smiling picture-book woods
Content as the smell
of a pretty girl's
warm neck.

Shepherd's Delight

And we shall shout & roar &
throw our spears at the sun

and know that nobody matters
& nothing cares

We sell our wares
to be the one

To know that all that was
& ever is & willing

Hangs like a fluttering flower
that goads abyss from steep cliff face

In this perfect, screaming moment
when all your universe

Teeters, totters
hangs in the balance--
of an idea.

Servitude was born
in curriculum's classroom
yet
freedom exists in a book.

In the schoolyard, it's up to you.

The Chrysalis
of exodus
Has passed o'er us
The terminus
& fountain well-known
Of future bliss
& reminisce
& random hell
Has passed

Golden piss
A fountain kiss
Of smell
through pipes, tanks, flows
Hiss
To chemical well
To rivers' lips
Has passed

Into sweaty suns abyss
to fluffy fist
Filial abacus

(Continued)

Falling tinkles knell
Porous cradle held
In cavernous ventriloquist
It has passed

Rolls to the reservoir
Poured to parched us
Oasis in a glass
To living terminus
Has passed

All life & death & birth in fits
Its reasoning sits
'Tween & 'twixt
Glass & piss
& I can tell cos I have passed
(From dusted sand to dusty glass)

Fly flew through my door
Poor hide chews glue pied
Pantry sentry dog agog
Fog-flogged elementary Gantry
Wall crawled craving
Pawing pawed halls hungry
Munchies scream cream crunchies
Dog food, glued sog
But beggars 'n choosy fly feels woozy
Emaciated fly flies, flew
Two pies, dry, unfaced with taste
Swoops barking air to plunder
Stoops garden chair to conquer

When Sand Dust Dies

Daybreak
Scatter of birds
Morning stirs

Possessed
Mother
Murders
A lucid dream

Giving reality
A self-consciousness
Even sobriety
Cannot find

Sensation of being
Cold & lost
70s Iron Curtain apartment complex
Swimming out of a faint

Momentary captive
In a foreign land
& it's hostile.

Lost in London

Maelstrom hailstorm
Bedroom window lights
Burn out
Into black nothing.
City streets swoon,
Swept into silent, soft slumber
& all but me
will be reborn
from shank's night mare
& spared
    & shorn.

Maelstrom hailstorm.
Nomad of night
& Mornings stillborn fawn.

Everything we say is a Cliche

Two Nubian neanderthals
Plucked from stone-faced ennui
as jewel embossed skylight harkened.
A cerebral smart, fosters fledgling revery.
Dung pile peppered savannah darkened.
The first, a hirsute type,
Amidst primordial clicks of conflicting flint
With puzzled sighs of apelike awe aripe,
didst grunt with neolithic etiquette
"How can the universe be infinite?"

Moist burning raindrops
Tap, touch & tingle,
the tortured tickle
Of that wide-eyed giggle.

My subtle insinuation
& soft contrived humility
the very definition
of flattering futility.

Once, down by the market place
In early morning's weary face
I met the meaning of yearning
On an empty, breakfastless soul

Then stomach thrown churning
Pleading the emergence
Of a wombed, rescuing hole
But breath & heartbeat

David & Goliath
Never fought;
The crushed relief
Her inattention brought.

Birthrights

As of Moses in the bible
A floating breath of silence
withdrew the waves of noise
To let forth
soft, fluid strumming
Unthinkable poise
ingenuity
gushing out chords of heavenly melody
Contorted face & eyes
replaying the cherub's last reprise
Hendrix, white Fender, & red sash too,
finding & doing what he was born to do.

Feminine form in a masculine frame
A favela dweller inspires the people's game
A perfect expression of sport's vital role
The free expression of mind, body & soul
Supernatural moments
of sublime simplicity
A team all-enveloped by youthful felicity
Pele, emblazoned in yellow & blue

(continued)

finding & doing what he was born to do.

Poor Polish peasant bears the bite
of mean winter's grip
numbed by a life that went nowhere quick
Subliminal the chessboards cry
A life lost in the blind spot of an eye
Skating it's corner
he never got warmer
He coulda been something if only he knew
failing to find what he was born to do.

The judge sneezes, squeezes the gavel &
finishes

the sentence, full stop.

The smiles & laughs at the lies

in his mind.

Pines from the accused

shocked & bemused

Sentences a thousand year stare

Through eyes quaking in a chair

A life lost in the loophole of a lie

He fit the script

Now reads the story

An unhappy minority

To a kangaroo jury.

Moody Restless Fever

Tired faces, Stale smoke,
Dried spit, Time to go.

Itching feet, Moody mind,
The goldfish bowl redefined.

The sky again
Reeks clear with grey,
clung too long
another day

Rank cider broods inside my veins
Fingers tapping for the call
Rented smoke snarls to escape

Take the high road out
while life's in spate
Go while you've
the wherewithal.

Sublime music & voices all around

(Continued)

Dry ice fury softly smoulders
Torment coils me into a flake
Pleading for that one clean break
I've got a moody, restless fever
& it ain't going away.

To The River

Through visions of dead, dark night
My mind, it races to my muse's shoulder
Oh heavens! What a wondrous sight!
Empty places, grassy pews
Soft breeze pleas me hold her

When we were young in sunkissed bliss
Addressed you baited through glassy tear
You cushioned woes of fish we missed
your living heartbeat on it flows
Times passed that's now an era

Over & Back

Spacing into a thousand-yard stare
I find,
As beautiful as the seven deadly sins
Entwined
Swimming out of the cavernous
Realms of there & then
Concentration clutching
For the last dew-drop of paradise

Before
The backwash of the senses
Carries you crestfallen
Back
to the cold, closed realities of the
here & now, again.

A Cyclical Sickness

Hollow school bells din
Balance scale o't'weeks arrived
The cornerstone of blissful grin
Last weekend once more relived
Uniformity discarded
Examinations soft retarded
Race to town,
Purchase drink,
Open mouths,
Out-loud think.
Church hill & other choices
Against a wall of urine, voices
Sharp chill of highland night
Greets the glow of vodka's bite
Cigarettes for those without
A schoolyard of appropriation
On B'sloe's outdoor social couch
Hosts ephemeral conversation
Confrontation, replication
& of course, conciliation
until all roaring residents do vacate
---off again for an institutional date.

The Fox & The Grouse

Fixed point rock
defines boundaries
& the vast limitless expanse
of conquest.
At this point

Spiritual blood vein
River
offloads in
content caterpillar-crawl undulation.
An unconscious parade.

Clothing of far bank
fishing
boys
kills timelessness
& creates an era.

Thin whispered rustle of reeds.
All-knowing insect eyes
peer through green thicket
at savage destinies.

(Continued)

Hushed heartbeat stampede
stirred in the bird
Unbreasts its beak
& unpreens the premise
of a natural death.

Cuts upwards
& knifes air
in silent shrill alert
splits atoms
sharp as eagle talons
to attention

Wishing wide-eyed chicks
to saving grace
of silence
beady eyed
& floundering.

In heart beat's hold
tries to arraign
arrange

(Continued)

random rustles
into coherent ponderous danger.

Ancient African drumbeats descend
Hunter & hunted
Primordial contest of wile
Insane foreplay
of natural coupling.

Stage
Ampitheatre
Gladatorial manoueverings
(Primitive presentation,
destiny's diorama)

Terrible neighbour bird plea
desperately deranged
calling harsh discord
into tense quietude.

Nervous hunter
Fox frozen

(Continued)

in self-conscious stupor
Aware
the daily rite of passage

& burden of victory
in this terrible seduction
& cursing
nature's sympathetic bias

through subtle clues
scent wind carried
& swaying reeds
urging escape.

Solemn trampled procession,
movements of murderous momentum.

Islence

If memory's a cabinet
filed
by well-meaning angels

Then You
crawled into a ball
a wall
& made a stranger.

To other-seeking eyes
under missing Teuton skies
lost & lamed ya, tossed & tamed ya
cost & claimed ya

Back into a shell
Like just anybody else---
To a stranger.

Blacksmith in cobbled stench
caring nursemaid of the hoof
Horse obedient
(kills sheep counting time)
Nay one not to notice
this bizarre human fetish
& leather-aproned
forges into the future
smith of words that sweat
the black unyielding clink of steel.

You're Real

Into a sea
A dream
Barefoot in a mountain stream
Drunk
Half-asleep
Skinnydippin' in the deep
To hear a piece of music for the first time
know you'll always get that shiver
Event as nostalgia, while it's happening
Eyes til cry a laughing tear
old photographs
first fumbling sex
last line of an amazing book
first dance with a new drug
liquorice
smell of a naked baby
the sound of a strange accent
that you can't quite place
sense of onrushing summer
first drag when you're a 'non-smoker'
a mountain-top roar
Echoes
a beautiful sunshower

(Continued)

becoming a Mammy or Daddy
the thrill of fear

a sweating sunshine beer

A feeling not quite real
like the creaming of a reel
your reel

Tunes
Croons
Tombs
Helium balloons
Universal swoons
Boredom
Burns
A worker's wage
Rancour rocks
In Monday morning's cage

Enniscrone Stream

When nature green & blue
forms covenant & living union
bridal bearers ere night of sparkling haze
& waters hum whispering tarns in the morning's dew
washing the faces of their stony neighbours
friends for a flash
sylph of silence, how she seduces
before life calls ever onwards
crumbling mortar brick protectors
slip dark aegis
cool in the swoony slumber of smiling sun
Fish tickle glass transparency
Loitering in the suspended motion of a crested jewel
brown, green fresh scents in essence
the glow of stirring conversation
Autumn's whisper ponderous
in the glint of each & every baby droplet
The paradox of life & death
playing together
lives in the dying breath
of moody weather.
All life lolls luxurious

(Continued)

All life locked
Behind a seal
of bubbling garrulous silence
Pure as an iceberg in a sunshower.

Untold Epitaph (micro)

Sun shine shone.
Snoozy summers day.

Wimbledon TV time
Tennis courts trampled
at the river
beside the bridge

Swimmers in the scummy Suck
Vied with fishing lines
old boots, & ducks

Mishit backhand smash
Slices skywards
Out of court settlement
---I'll get it

We see Spud Murphy in a spin

A coal sack into silt sank
---Ring an ambulance, or the pigs
just so somethin', Quick!

Mental patient went impatient
In the institution
The great escape

---I'm not goin t'the pigs, they're
after me anyways!
---Just fucken go!

The flurry of rumour
Wildfire
on an empty Summer's day
Chinese whispers
Rumours run a racket

The sunshine splits, &
Stark cloud knits the sky

People out from under stones
Seem to crawl
& into a crowd, fall

Twice entertainment to concern

Time forgotten as a tennis ball

Cars slow to a squinting standstill
to speculate
& talk at tea time.

Sackcloth soul in a sack
Tween a rock & a hard place
Where now
the empty face?

Birds swooped downstream
'scaping memos of mortality

Two girls giggle & scream
water down their togs streams
----sshh......shut up!

Summer sinks into stomach pits

We into the water waded
Martin Murray topless trudged
& made it

("Oh, I can't look" one woman said,
& looked)
to the purple shell
of a soul in absentia

Swollen gargles & smells
as a leaky boot

Men helped carry the corpse
With the cold concentration
Of non-thinking

Cackles from the carried corpse
Eyelids flapping
Fear forever in a moment
In the frame of frozen faces

Ambulance siren swirls

False banter in the aftermath
instant amnesia
of a blithe soul, lost
as a tennis ball.

Let's be chieftains

With blood red hand
Of roughshod Indians
In a mystic land
(Your school reader you must forgive
Fionn & Cuchulainn did really live)
& kill all shadow
we'll run so quick
but not to break
a single stick.

Bodhrans beat
Bones
Underneath the
Fairy stones

Foggy green plants
Itself on ancient brow

Kingdoms pass & kings allow

Vicissitudes of time & space

sing in the gods' unblinkered grace

& crannogs deep
with buttered churns
hiding peat filligreed urns

mock & oh!

In Gaelic, flow
Flutter in the early dew
                    have the crack
but pass away
under eastern sons
attack anew

Across the waves of centuries
absorbed
in the culture
of native sentries

& girls playing harps
of fiery red
while mushroomed Druids

sing along with the dead
sad ballads skate wild skies

wild wolves in wide woods
with their tails
of the seanchai
who remembers thee

the river is a mirror
& friendly
on our shivers back
to god in a bush

so lush
with lore
our ancestors swore

& talks like our sister
stream of whispers
& for us in ways to mother Eireann asks
of druids & myths & pagan days of Celtic past
(Can she remember
her sow in November?)

invisible bard
the night still rambles
leaves embroidery woven
in the brambles

that still lurks
in the ring of trees
with answers swaying
in the breeze.

Girl crashes into me on street
Fumbles for a dog-eared book
Left hanging on the ground
An unplanned meet;
our blue eyes greet
the apex of a thousand generations.

Poem Written on the Street
(When Saharan sand blew over Dublin. Mar 1998)

Professional city streets
Got more ties
Than eyes that greet

Girls unfurl in fashioned flocks
In smiling swirls
Under beaded locks

Brash boys outbid & boast each other
Townie taches that
Still fear their mothers

Daylight nightclub haunts
'members only'
neon lights never looked so lonely

& couples in a hand's embrace
see what they need in another's face
the dove of love is sweet deceit

The blind busker basks
In all he's seen
& how the fuck do blind men dream?

With no other faces on which to try
The flautist's face
Never learned to lie

Tired pedestrian walks
On bored dog's leash
The pig farmer's daughter would like the quiche

Househunters chase flats just outta reach
'Flats to let' for two
“a half bed each, the floor for you!”

as pigeons pilot
sunburned shit
the juggler of Hamlyn pipes in Grafton's pit

as forests hide
on bookshop shelves

readers over covers delve

Young boys handless
eye the smut
which, at a height, halts their guts

Urchins bargain at trader's stalls
arguing hands
In pockets that stole

As apples are whored by peppy paupers
The meat is sold
By their deed polled daughters

All rush & hurry in ev'ry ants urban eye
All fret & flurry in the
Atlantis of timetabled elsewhere

Trans-port boats enwave
The pirateers of produce
Export shores

Where squalls send their will on a seagull's wing

skating the edge
on blue concave peel

but Today,
Orange sails from the sky
Through windows at workers wishful

& criminal eyes
& parks & greens & gold tinged hair
& statues & buildings & trees & air

& I'm happy
soft silt Saharan sand
chose the car (of my dreams)

on which to land
It sailed the seven seas for me
Swam simooming breeze for me

& I am blessed
like all the rest
for living in a life less ordinary

(continued)

Because of thee
Sweet sand
of a dusky, dusty land

Be thee Yorrick's bollock
or
Great Alexander's hand.

Pygmalion stale in eon swig
blue funked he
black knotted me
Criss-crossed moments
in the misunderstanding of existence
Persistence & dappled diplomacy
clasp the phonecy of resistance
to past & 'Jonesing'
On a grand scale
our duets wail
fueled
the next world war
(In the soft lapping
I feel a mental slapping sting
on Oriental butterfly's flapping wing)

Flashback

Bittersweet symphony.
Brown, orange, red & green
honey & clove memory
in sunny September's slipstream.

Nostalgia strife
when unappreciated bike
cycled through B'sloe
in the misery dictionary of days
I thought's never go

Seeing seniors
of the 3 schools
messing
in that short sweet interlude
Tween schools clothes & home

& that strange sensation
of that blond brat
a-chafing at the tie

(Continued)

top-button longterm unemployed

bunking longer lunch breaks
smoking in the woods
answering back
& swerving through the busy theatre of society
& main st

spawns a teardrop between the eyes

My fraught nape
missing the days
& ploys
once fought to escape.

Compass blunted
life unjointed
aimless stunted
wherem I pointed?

Into the wilderness
of security
obscurity
son the trough
til elder'ness
insurity
of a safe wife
chafe at life

Where I shoulda been all along
Get me there, on a Judas prayer
no silent swear in mean throng
no coulda-been song

That boy was born to die
Aye, he was
moist in the velvet mellow cloud
of futurity

the invisible shroud, blissless
vanishes listless to his touch
w/ saddened surety
& hoist, banishes
the shel*ved* cloistered grand divisible
of present clutch

To fiery blazing bur*ned* boat Valhalla
I see in the tomorrow of today
gazing chur*ned* coat favela
immutable decay
drifting to a slow-slung death
thrifting you a clove clung breath

Life's been so easy
falling into future peasy
Senescent strife
of signposted misdirection
galling tutor & midwife
of an eternal suitor
in the voids reflection

Why do I do just what I do?

Blowing smoke & spark anew
drink ensoaked unhappiness
& weary through-and-through
Hanger-on and hangerover
of something new
turning clover
Into the wilderness
of security, obscurity
don the trough til elder'ness
insurity
of a safe wife
chafe at life.

Compass blunted
life unjointed
aimless stunted
wherem I pointed?

Stoning of the Leper

One winter's day
Walking my dog through the
domesticated wilderness
of a muddied pasture
adjacent a vibrant housing estate
my trusty wolf-wannabe
spies a wasting leprous rabbit
on a grassy verge
a thousand million miles
from the concrete physics
in which she resides.

Angry clouds race an Arctic sky
trees applaud obedient
fearful to defy.
Soft bovine excrement
thistles, nettles, thorns
prophesise a devilment
an eerie chill forewarns.

Liquid jewels shine in unison

before us, out wavelike as we walk
dark, dusky sky of November
a shimmering, glassy chorus
a rented living pearl on eve'ry stalk & blade
Ere plodding size elevens
destroy the moist charade.

Jessie's ears
for that's the only name she hears
prick & quiver, all attent
her cold nose wriggles, struggles
to expose exotic living scent.

On her lips saliva jiggles
her appetite's been whet
crying out, incipient
a morbid scene is set.

Plucked from a passing moment
& frozen framed
a picture of suspended animation
I realise things have changed
man & dog

primordial relations
hunters & gatherers of glutton
now domestically deranged.

The Age of Aquarius

The Mappa Mundi
The soul of the world
I feel it
When unfurled
In fleeing rabbits
& frothing hounds
That instinct programmed from ancestral bones
than ever hunger or anty mounds.....

In crashing sea & shivering foams
Or green-eyed children's lilting glee
In stirring songs & fiery poems
in roughshod forest with sheltered lees
in stories spake where dandy dallies
Where mossy mountains reverence valleys
In golden glowing antiquities, deliverance
through childlike minds
A worker's wage, safe shuttered blinds
on final page

lazy weekends
in the smoky sounds of small hour bars
Priorities blend
In pursuing police & racing cars
In budding leaves & ripening berries
In royal seas & scarlet cherries
In citron sun & sanguine worries
In rosebud lips, in hazel eyes
in slothfulness, in enterprise
in pangs of hunger
Tween lovers warm
in life rent asunder
in more life born
in knowledge lost & found & lost
in drunken fights, in old compost
in soft acceptance of lifes long night
in laughter & in tears
in choler & in fears
in rivers flow a restless jewel
in painted birds on flapping wings
in ev'ry eye there lives a fool
& in the beggars who are kings
in crumbling, conquered Rome

in terrorists who try
in dusted bones, their legacy tomes
in ancient Apollo idols eye
in murderous plans & straw liced stables
in shaman's trance & childhood fables
in maddening gale & tremulous torrent
in whisp'ring spring & icy current
in wind-swept scents & harrowing squeals
in the hunters morn & swaying fields
in insect crawling concrete slabs
& graffiti canvased peer approval
in speeding smart-assed driven cabs
& in sewerage removal.....

The Mappa Mundi
to a million men unfolds
with a million windows
to its soul.

* * * *

Universe eternal & limitless
as a drop

in the ocean

of an ocean

in the drop

of another Universe

(soft translucent collusion)

Fluid Flowing Swimming

existence

Watery & Slippery

Signposts of definition

Borders Boundaries Divisions

in our Universe

dance in carefree

ebb & flow

like

seaman sperm

on the go

* * * * *

Fell the drum beat
of ancient tribal savannah
Spears sharpen
life or death
in the tasting of
a new found fruit.
The wheel.
The flint
into fire.
Stone into metal.
Grunts
to chants
to words
to language
remember?

& the vast lottery of ancestral union

until
Moment of coupling explosion.
Chaos theory, if you microcosm
to the sperm & egg.
Another Universe

on the head of a pin.
Fusion squared.
Electric spark
the soul creates.
Umbilical discord
backing 1st scream vocals
& into this howling world
is thrown (in at the deep end of
the goldfish bowl)
((begat when bubble burst
& out was shat))

In the wombdream
bloody vision you cried
in the newborn moment.

Journey Vision Venture

The dawn has passed & to die is cast.

The young soul opens the sensory book
& is left to wander, to search & to look.....

* * * * *

The new teacher
slid into the classroom
nervous smile slips
into deranged spasmed twitch.

A single frame frozen
a *look*
cold solemn
worry
fear
scared either of us (his students)
or
his worthiness
in the role of all prophets
as disciple
imparting the accepted wisdoms
of ancient teachers.

Tries to look into our souls
for empathy or compassion
but is stopped

in his tracks
at our eyes
cold solemn judgmental
& sucking him
of information.

Teachers are premature ejaculations---
leaning forward but craning backwards
a kind of unfinished tidal wave

Us students
ride upon the crest of a fledgling wave
& he/she imparts fearful
words & lessons
of caution
& dutiful warnings
as he/she is carried
back on the slipstream swash
Back
to the next fledgling wave,
authority his badge,
prize, consolation for cowardice
in stepping back

No full monty to the beach
chanting: 'Thus far & no further'

to the vast radiant
beach party quest
for knowledge & discovery

Teacher when studying is a disciple
& only becomes Lord w/ an eager audience.

Teachers are a limitation
in themselves
& in their blinkering
of young minds
in how they
receive
discern
appreciate
the fluid burning wheel
of knowledge, atmosphere
understanding & surrounding

Yet no-one escapes

as I scold my young cousin
---eating cake from a fan---
which was serving more than adequately
as plate & serviette

& shout at him
cos That's not the way you do it
Not what it's for
Not what you were Taught

Here I am teacher
poisoning his young mind

False teachers, unelected, abound in every human mound

*   *   *   *   *

Anythings possible
Oh charismatic sky of summer
Everything is colour
& natures singing mummers

* * * * *

In The Heydays of Summers, I

Freshly cut grass
A sensual simoom
Its inky breath
Permeates
Exuberant
Golden
Children
Radiate from the
Son of earth
He,
---A bloody orange---
Melts
On her eyes in

The lazy garden.

Slower shadows slide
Melodious air
& faster footballs fly
To fights.
Temperature tempered

& lost in the fall
Of shimmering night.

Lowing lawnmowers.
Suncream, sandy feet.
Bar-b-q messenger smoke implores
A blackened charcoal treat
Timeless
In its tasty transience.

Relative theories on times pass
Relatively useless
tanning by a flapping clothes line
Fanning

Competitive school hours fought
Calendar gorging
Father, ever forging
Fay of time
Appetite felled
He now reclines
To the beat of living nature
Whats his is mine

& alls sublime

The clay-minted aeon offered us
Is a duelling, growling gauntlet
'gin sloth & 'stalgia sickly sweet
But bliss on this breath
Should be flaunted
& exalted & revered
Adventure skating the cusp of here

So much for
Childhood.....happiness.....innocence.....lost
To a tragic romantic urn
Pathetic poetic ascetics
Though swallows fly
They do return

Burst football
Tombstone, grains
Eggtimer rent
But creeping soul
Can happ'ly groan
To a sudden childhood spent.

* * * * *

Summer warms the soul reborn.

The mad & the children.......as I was young & easy
under an apple bough........

Let your child
out to play
Return to secret summer hideaway
(Where innocence anoints us in splendour
& preserves in us the fresh miracle
of surprise)

Come into my secret womb garden
Let rose petals play
tickle your face
& flutter dancing
in the breeze.

Come
Pale, uncertain stranger

dripping the smell
of cold, grey emptiness
Face luxuriance w/
unruffled smile
Let tired eyes
squinting
liquify & settle
round black borders
& let a thin grey film
fall
cleansing
Come
& let slide the restless
wanderings of humanity

At Last
we've found what we're
looking for
enmeshed in daisy chains
& sunny bird song
& hopskotched gaiety
& green knee patches
& dirty fingernails

on mucky hands

Come
climb w/ me
into the paradise
of my tree
(where alone I always
felt in good company)
that competes w/
the blue sky
& w/ silence

Secret garden
where my name
& memory meet
in crude penknife signature
Come
back to the days
when reality & fantasy
fought furiously
for control
of a childs mind
(& fantasy rules ok)

Colourful cloister
where the world's news
meant nothing to me
except North East West South

* * * * *

This Summer
The sun pours down like honey
In golden soft procession.

The Scheme was a dream
I didn't mean.

Human ants cluster urban mounds.
Crowds dissemble church Colosseum
rejoicing the freedom
from an hour's uncertain devotion.
Lovers handheld blossom
building the leafy nostalgia
of romantic memories
that'll warm frail joints
in the Wintry wilderness of their lives.

Saving for the rainy day.

*   *   *   *   *

Summer of our madness
our worries wintry wallow;
warm we wooze
Waterfalls & wonder
fear of getting caught
detained, in the knowledge
possession
that transient is our
freedom.

But don't talk to me about this age
when its old enough to drink

A glorious summer
watered down with the sad, sloe
awareness
of times pass
& dispersions into money-making
manhood.

* * * * *

If a picture
Can paint a thousand words
Then an action
Can taint a thousand cords

Only when he broke a string
did his music strike a chord

Deep water still runs.

The Fear:
Buried alive
Panting towards death
totally immobile
watching yourself
Scream
in your own ears
In a coffin of mirrors.

The eye
sharpest knife

softest bed
faintest voice
A window, not a mirror.

Daisy chains, cannibal lesbians
cropped hair circumnavigates
Split ends
of the Universe
Gone Fission

Crows seem to be getting
more fearless
every day.

Tobacco clouds
sensation's radar
as Heat
inflames temperament.

* * * * *

Magpie strolls in
handpawed window current glide

Splits my daydream side-to-side
& slate-grey beak cuts air
w/ black-white splash forebodes
like flying flotsam 'thout a care
in private airspace code.

What jinx is found
from myth that festers
in loins unbound
of occulted ancestors?

*   *   *   *   *

Trawler fishermen
the pirates of politics wheel
Skating the edge
on blue concave peel.
(Squalls send their will
on a seagulls wing)

By nightfall, graveyard pails
A swarming site
W/ revamped tales of
Released delight.

Life: unending concentration of scenes
arranged to placate human egoic sensibilities
& create tenses.

* * * * *

Night club anthem
bellows & billows
Ushered out
by their private army
Ringing ears, hoarse voice
greet our passing
the threshold
into the chill.

Darkness envelops.
Taxis. Screams.
Smoke sails a starry shudder.
The police us do police,
higgledy-piggledy.
Night stirrings
enfold, unfold
Then fold

The hive dies.

At night
the streets hold whispered
wisdom & secrets
in blown-breath
salt & vinegar chips
& boys & girls
in empty promises
& little white lies.

Everywhere there are hives
of activity
stinging the backside
of the city night
w/ laughter
& lust
& looks
& smoke heavenwards
chanting prophesies in the vain hope
of killing the great guardian angel
daylight
that great overcoat of secrecy

& acceptable behaviour.

The night carries w/ it
a sense of theatre--
merry
revellers
jig, skip & dance
the kerbs,
weaving costumes of warmth
in the black of night.

In these moments
we're searching, yearning
to create a memorable past
in the drunken present
& the vast promissory note
of the future.

The Tunnel
a pilgrimage of habit
a sort of candle
you touch & get burned by.
The blister bubbles in

the birth of regret foreboding
wasted
money & energy
the liquid pus
is the vain, defiant hope
of breaking free
of its templed thrall
& never returning

until the next time
& the next
& the next

Never further from next weekend
Fantasising along the streets
in sleeps warm rapture
all around arms o' nod
stroke a soft yawn
a ticklish tension
in the bones
shopfronts slide by
& everywhere
is restless & wanting

(Sunday morn is nothing at all
but an iron helmet
thats too small
a wheezing voice
& speckled wall)

under drunkenesses veiled cloak
safe, womb-warm
in the protective knowledge
of forgetfulness
& the lost lucid dream
of morning afters memory....

(Memory is a cabinet
filed by well-meaning angels)

There is contentedness
in idleness
until awareness steps in.

People spit at the cold-shivered
ground, but know the night

is accommodating
---a silken shine to
dark mysteries, secrecies
& amber ruby metamorphosis.

The looser pubs, dark & cool & shady
where underage types
give ill-gotten employment
to a bar stools owner.

The boy ahead
treads the boards
hoping to wend his way
into certainty
that the girl wants him

The girl ahead
treads the boards
eager to please
w/ colluding, careful giggles
hoping to wend her way
into certainty
that the boy wants her

& later feast on each others hot desire.

* * * * *

The police pepper the great pitch.

Never to know complete
wild abandon again
once that 1st photo in the
uniform is taken.

(Isn't it strange & have you
ever noticed
how different you look
in your mirror
& in a photo?)

Carry a gun in self-defence
Warm in the pocket
it creates a shallow confidence
but offends
& creates abnormal aggression

in the carrier

of this abnormal
insecure new disease
of the urban 90s.

(The gun is just an extension
of murderous eyes intention)

* * * * *

The future is written
on ancient tablets of stone
in invisible ink.

Like young children giving the answer
the parent wants to hear
the cells under the microscope
arrange themselves to please
the scientist's eye.
A charade, a holographic dance,
a seduction of observer
& observed

you cannot be objective
there's no way to stand outside the game.
You are always within the experiment.

The scientist tries to verify the soul's existence
Should not the soul verify the scientists existence?
Measuring the depth of death with a ruler.

* * * * *

Depth of Death

Corpse pales innocent to the ceiling
A pointer to it's hiding place
people weeping selfishly
stare into an empty face

Blinded: more certain than day
following night is life hosting death,
a harbinger of earthly flight
& bittersweet regret

Their fear of final breath
mirrors *dep*thed faith
a renaissance of uncertainty

when nature all negates

Inside, creations crossing guard replies
accost its foetal child to the other side
born out of deadlock
the mini-dream of life has died

Has the pallid temple
deserted by it's mortal hero
shuffled off the slumber line
or returned to absolute zero?

* * * * *

I am all-powerful.
I am you is we.

I possess the power to conquer & overwhelm all partitioned creeds, beliefs, religions, disbeliefs & philosophies in one clean swoop. I possess the power & hold dominion over all cosmic, psychic & physical conundrums.

I clasp the lifeblood of all existence in my hands.
Trained between my eyes,

Pull the trigger.

Ultimate out-of-body experience.

This is power, raw & pure:

Make me a martyr of my own deep searching questions.

As the shot rings out I become your all-knowing God since in that smoky second, that Universal intersection, where deja-vus blend & meet at the crossroads, I am thrown headlong into total unlearned understanding.

'I just know'

Off my tongue'll trip elementary answers to questions you could never comprehend.

Using the lock to open the key.

In the gilt-edged hour,

catapulted from my, his, the corpse

Depart w/ certain uncertainties & a hint of regret.

I'll be that thief-rapist-land law likened sinner at Columbus' heel who,

waltzing & squinting the blue jeweled afterbirth of another age,

thinks & links frying pan & fire

(like being born

or 1st school morn)

Life: 'the shit that happens while you're making plans'.

Preparations for return to the womb.

A nursery.

A test.

Rite of passage.

Incoherent riddle.

End of the beginning

& beginning of the end.

The chicken & the egg

coming home to seed.

Dreams in sleep: coded mysteries.

Tiny excerpts of eternity.

A deja-vu we can't remember?

Concession for the eternal circus tent.

* * * * *

In the netherworld, do unhappy souls curse eternal exile?

Mystic traveller, I see us prisoners to another law,

lolling in the loamy void

(Without fluids

For bodily treasures
We'll screw the stars
& shoot their treasures)
Harold Norse

I'll amass a cache, a crew
& will the heavens storm
break free the shackles
of its templed thrall
& challenge in duel
the ephemeral dictator,
this inter-dimensional despot.
(& theology tips its hat to this tyrant)

& w/ all fight & fury fought
will choose the elixir
of my own eternal rest
& be blest.

& golden flowing vapours
toing & froing in unconscious warmth
happiness of emotional couplings
spontaneous & for all eternity

will be our sentenced bliss

& we'll be cool droplets
in a sun-soaked sea
bubbles on the breeze
of whimsy & felicity
dancing on the snug lap of eternities crest
the worlds womb

Death is the alchemy of transformation
like the diver steely
land
air
water.

A mere metamorphosis
the mad last writhings of the shell
Slipped of its soul
Like a fumbling caterpillar
Released w/ wings on freedoms flight
Transformation
into beauty brimmed content
from crawling conflict

The sweet ascent.

& before that 1st & final flight
take life by its cuffing scruff
w/ fists of fire
& live uncompromisingly
& live a full lifes life

*   *   *   *   *

Not
in a dark spiderous secrecy
shall I go
wringing the hands of ghostly confessors
shivering in a clock tock-ticking room
of feeble groans
lifes movie mulls & memory moans
sad sickly flesh on bones like looms
askew the hollow-shone moon.

Oft in times of curious wonder
I've contemplated the power of self plunder
& in that hour

not from loathing, or for attentions flower
but to sunder Christianities
clothing & contention
of eternal life, a fourth dimension
by this the ultimate of vanities
---a vessel to the perpetual pension

But in case I'm right
& as lifes in spate & able
I'll hesitate from maggots
plate & table

I want to go out in a fiery blaze
No slow-slide shuffling
A-shooting from the hip I'll phase
no weak or senile muddled muffling
Its here I'll ransack Edens garden
Splode on summers strongest chime
Ere jellied brain can set & harden
No compromise to grindstone time.

* * * * *

Universe eternal & limitless

as a drop
in the ocean
of an ocean
in the drop
of another Universe

(soft translucent collusion)

Fluid   Flowing   Swimming
existence
watery & slippery

Signposts of definition
Borders   Boundaries   Divisions

in our Universe

dance in carefree
ebb & flow
like seaman sperm
on the go

& outta this howling world is thrown,

in at the deep end
    smiles the soul.

THE END

www.ingramcontent.com/pod-product-compliance
Ingram Content Group UK Ltd.
Pitfield, Milton Keynes, MK11 3LW, UK
UKHW020222250726
13967UKWH00001B/135
9 781291 734447